AF454241

To Celebrate

____

____

Date

____

THANK YOU FOR COMING.

Let's celebrate!

Guest Name

Wishes & Messages

Email/Phone

Guest Name

Wishes & Messages

Email/Phone

Guest Name

Wishes & Messages

EMAIL/PHONE ___________________________

Guest Name

____

Wishes & Messages

____

____

____

____

____

____

EMAIL/PHONE ____

Guest Name

Wishes & Messages

Email/Phone

Guest Name

Wishes & Messages

EMAIL/PHONE

Guest Name

Wishes & Messages

EMAIL/PHONE

Guest Name

Wishes & Messages

Email/Phone

Guest Name

Wishes & Messages

Email/Phone

Guest Name

Wishes & Messages

Email/Phone

Guest Name

Wishes & Messages

EMAIL/PHONE

Guest Name

Wishes & Messages

Email/Phone

Guest Name

Wishes & Messages

Email/Phone

Guest Name

Wishes & Messages

Email/Phone

Guest Name

Wishes & Messages

EMAIL/PHONE

Guest Name

Wishes & Messages

EMAIL/PHONE

Guest Name

Wishes & Messages

Email/Phone

Guest Name

Wishes & Messages

Email/Phone

Guest Name

____

Wishes & Messages

____

____

____

____

____

____

EMAIL/PHONE
____

Guest Name

Wishes & Messages

E
Email/Phone

Guest Name

Wishes & Messages

EMAIL/PHONE

Guest Name

Wishes & Messages

Email/Phone

Guest Name

Email/Phone

Guest Name

Wishes & Messages

Email/Phone

Guest Name

Wishes & Messages

EMAIL/PHONE

Guest Name

Wishes & Messages

Email/Phone

Guest Name

Wishes & Messages

Email/Phone

Guest Name

Wishes & Messages

Email/Phone

Guest Name

____

Wishes & Messages

____

____

____

____

____

____

Email/Phone
____

Guest Name

Wishes & Messages

EMAIL/PHONE

Guest Name

Wishes & Messages

Email/Phone

Guest Name

Wishes & Messages

Email/Phone

Guest Name

Wishes & Messages

Email/Phone

Guest Name

Wishes & Messages

Email/Phone

Guest Name

Wishes & Messages

Email/Phone

Guest Name

Wishes & Messages

Email/Phone

Guest Name

Wishes & Messages

Email/Phone

Guest Name

Wishes & Messages

Email/Phone

Guest Name

Wishes & Messages

Email/Phone

Guest Name

Wishes & Messages

Email/Phone

Guest Name

Wishes & Messages

Email/Phone

Guest Name

Wishes & Messages

Email/Phone

Guest Name

Wishes & Messages

Email/Phone

Guest Name

Wishes & Messages

Email/Phone

Guest Name

Wishes & Messages

____

Email/Phone

Guest Name

Wishes & Messages

Email/Phone

Guest Name

Wishes & Messages

Email/Phone

Guest Name

Wishes & Messages

EMAIL/PHONE

Guest Name

Wishes & Messages

Email/Phone

Guest Name

Wishes & Messages

Email/Phone

Guest Name

Wishes & Messages

Email/Phone

Guest Name

Wishes & Messages

EMAIL/PHONE

Guest Name

Wishes & Messages

EMAIL/PHONE

Guest Name

Wishes & Messages

Email/Phone

Guest Name

Wishes & Messages

Email/Phone

Guest Name

Wishes & Messages

Email/Phone

Guest Name

Wishes & Messages

Email/Phone

Guest Name

Wishes & Messages

EMAIL/PHONE

Guest Name

Wishes & Messages

Email/Phone

Guest Name

Wishes & Messages

Email/Phone

Guest Name

Wishes & Messages

Email/Phone

Guest Name

Wishes & Messages

Email/Phone

Guest Name

Wishes & Messages

Email/Phone

Guest Name

Wishes & Messages

Email/Phone

Guest Name

Wishes & Messages

Email/Phone

Guest Name

Wishes & Messages

Email/Phone

Guest Name

Wishes & Messages

Email/Phone

Guest Name

Wishes & Messages

Email/Phone

Guest Name

Wishes & Messages

EMAIL/PHONE

Guest Name

Wishes & Messages

Email/Phone

Guest Name

Wishes & Messages

EMAIL/PHONE

Wishes & Messages

EMAIL/PHONE

Guest Name

Wishes & Messages

____

____

____

____

____

____

Email/Phone
____

Guest Name

Wishes & Messages

Email/Phone

Guest Name

Wishes & Messages

Email/Phone

Guest Name

Wishes & Messages

Email/Phone

Guest Name

Wishes & Messages

Email/Phone

Guest Name

Wishes & Messages

Email/Phone

Guest Name

Wishes & Messages

EMAIL/PHONE

Guest Name

Wishes & Messages

Email/Phone

Guest Name

Wishes & Messages

EMAIL/PHONE

Guest Name

____

Wishes & Messages

____

____

____

____

____

____

Email/Phone
____

Guest Name

Wishes & Messages

Email/Phone

Guest Name

Wishes & Messages

E

Email/Phone

Guest Name

Wishes & Messages

EMAIL/PHONE

Guest Name

Wishes & Messages

Email/Phone

Guest Name

Wishes & Messages

Email/Phone

Guest Name

Wishes & Messages

EMAIL/PHONE

Guest Name

Wishes & Messages

Email/Phone

Guest Name

Wishes & Messages

Email/Phone

Guest Name

Wishes & Messages

____

____

____

____

____

____

EMAIL/PHONE
____

Guest Name

Wishes & Messages

Email/Phone

Guest Name

____

Wishes & Messages

____

____

____

____

____

____

Email/Phone
____

Guest Name

Wishes & Messages

Email/Phone

Guest Name

Wishes & Messages

Email/Phone

Guest Name

Wishes & Messages

____

____

____

____

____

____

Email/Phone _______________________________

Guest Name

Wishes & Messages

Email/Phone

Guest Name

Wishes & Messages

Email/Phone

Guest Name

Wishes & Messages

✉ Email/Phone

Guest Name

Wishes & Messages

Email/Phone

Guest Name

Wishes & Messages

Email/Phone

Guest Name

Wishes & Messages

Email/Phone

Guest Name

Wishes & Messages

Email/Phone

Guest Name

Wishes & Messages

Email/Phone

Wishes & Messages

Email/Phone

Guest Name

Wishes & Messages

EMAIL/PHONE

NOTES & PHOTOS

NOTES & PHOTOS

NOTES & PHOTOS

NOTES & PHOTOS

GIFT LOG

Name / Email / Phone	Gift

GIFT LOG

Name / Email / Phone	Gift

GIFT LOG

Name /Email /Phone

Gift

GIFT LOG

Name /Email /Phone	Gift

GIFT LOG

Name / Email / Phone	Gift

GIFT LOG

Name / Email / Phone	Gift

GIFT LOG

Name / Email / Phone   Gift

www.ingramcontent.com/pod-product-compliance
Lightning Source LLC
LaVergne TN
LVHW080846240726
843527LV00052B/255